HOCKEY PUZZLERS
Offbeat Trivia for the Fan and the Fanatic

Bob Moll

Chicago, Illinois

For my family

Contents

CATEGORY 1

RULES

1

Is the goaltender allowed to play with a broken stick?

2

On a delayed offside, if the defensive team puts the puck in their own net without any contact from the other team, does the goal count?

3

If a player throws a stick and successfully blocks what would have been an empty net goal, what happens?

4

If a shot hits the post without the goaltender touching it and deflects away from the net, is it considered a shot on goal?

5

What is the consequence if a player other than the goaltender grasps the puck in the crease?

1

Yes, the goaltender is allowed to play with a broken stick. Postion players cannot play with broken sticks.

2

It is possible to score an "own goal" on a delayed off-side, so the goal counts.

3

It is not legal to throw a stick to block a puck, so the goal is awarded.

4

A puck that hits the post is not considered a shot on goal.

5

If a player other than the goaltender grasps the puck in the crease a penalty shot is awarded.

6

On a penalty shot, what happens if the goaltender leaves the crease prior to the shooting player touching the puck?

7

In a regular season game if regualtion time ends 4 on 4, how many players will be on the ice when the overtime period starts?

8

What is the diameter and height of an official hockey puck?

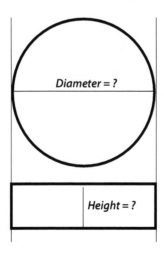

6

The shooting player, should he not score, will be allowed to shoot again.

7

The overtime would start with 3 on 3.

8

The diameter of a hockey puck is three inches and the height is 1 inch.

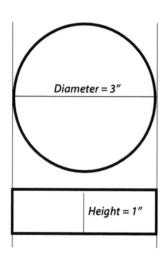

9

Identify three errors in the ice rink diagram below.

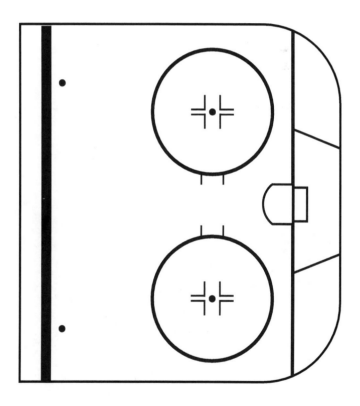

9

The correct diagram is shown below. The three errors in the prior diagram are as follows:

1. Face off dots should appear just outside the blue line, not inside the blue line.
2. Outer hash marks should appear on both sides of the face off circles.
3. The trapezoid should have the narrower side by the net and the wider side by the boards.

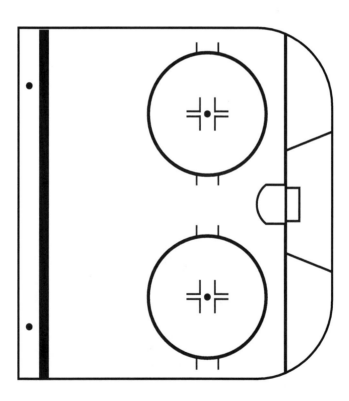

10

Are goaltenders allowed to cross their own blue line?

11

If a player gets two minor penalties together he would be assessed a double minor. Is it possible to get a triple minor?

12

How many players can dress for an NHL game?

13

Name two situations in which the referee (as apposed to a linesman) does the faceoff.

14

What happens if the goaltender plays the puck behind the net but outside of the trapezoid area?

15

What is the maximum number of players allowed on an NHL roster?

10

Yes, the goaltender can cross his own blue line but not the center ice red line.

11

It is possible to get a triple minor.

12

Twenty players can dress for an NHL game, 18 position players and 2 goaltenders.

13

The referee does the face off at the beginning of a period and after a goal.

14

If the goaltender plays the puck outside of the trapezoid area a minor penalty is assessed.

15

An NHL roster can have 23 players.

16

If the puck stops halfway on the goal line and half-way across the goal line, is it considered a goal?

17

If a player directs the puck into the net with a stick held above the cross bar, does the goal count?

16

The puck must be completely across the goal line to count as a goal. If any part of the puck is on the line, it is not a goal.

17

A puck redirected with a stick above the cross bar would not count as a goal should the puck go into the net.

CATEGORY 2

TEAMS

EAST	WEST
Boston Bruins	Anaheim Ducks
Buffalo Sabres	Arizona Coyotes
Carolina Hurricanes	Calgary Flames
Columbus Blue Jackets	Chicago Blackhawks
Detriot Red Wings	Colorado Avalanche
Florida Panthers	Dallas Stars
Montreal Canadiens	Edmonton Oilers
New Jersey Devils	Los Angeles Kings
New York Islanders	Minnesota Wild
New York Rangers	Nashville Predators
Ottawa Senators	San Jose Sharks
Philadelphia Flyers	St. Louis Blues
Pittsburgh Penguins	Vancouver Canucks
Tampa Bay LIghtning	Winnipeg Jets
Toronto Maple Leafs	
Washington Capitals	

18

If two Original Six teams meet in the Stanley Cup finals, which team is guaranteed to be one of the two?

19

Which expansion team of the six added in the 1967-68 season took the fewest number of years to win the Stanley Cup?

20

Excluding black and white, what is the most popular major color used in NHL uniforms?

21

Which double numbers (11, 22, 33, 44, 55, 66, 77, 88, 99) have been retired by at least one team?

22

Of the 30 NHL teams, how many have not won a Stanley Cup?

18

If two Original Six teams meet in the finals, the Chicago Blackhawks will be one of the teams as they are the only Original Six team in the West.

19

The Philadelphia Flyers were the first expansion team to win the cup. It took seven years, with them capturing the cup in the 1973-74 season.

20

Blue is most popular and is featured by 11 teams, red is second and is featured by 10 teams.

21

The numbers 11, 22, 33, 66, 77 and 99 have been retired by at lesast one team.

22

As of 2015, eleven teams out of 30 have yet to win a Stanley Cup.

23

Which US states have more than one NHL team?

24

Which teams have retired the number 1?

25

Of the five largest cities in the US, which one does not have an NHL team?

26

Are there more teams in the NHL or the NBA?

27

Of the 30 NHL teams, how many are named after animals?

23

California and New York each have three teams while Pennsylvania and Florida each have two.

24

The following teams have retired the number 1:

> Chicago Blackhawks
> Detroit Red Wings
> Minnesota Wild
> Montreal Canadiens
> New York Rangers
> Philadelphia Flyers

25

Houston is the 4th largest city but has no NHL team.

26

Both the NHL and NBA have 30 teams.

27

Seven teams are named after animals. They are:

> Anaheim Ducks
> Arizona Coyotes
> Boston Bruins
> Florida Panthers
> Pittsburgh Penguins
> San Jose Sharks
> Vancouver Canucks

28

Which team has retired the most numbers?

29

Which team has the word "Hockeytown" as part of its center ice logo?

30

Which team goes by the nickname the Bolts?

31

Which US team is located the furthest south?

32

Which team featuers three stars as part of its logo?

33

Which two teams feature a single star as a part of their logos?

28

The Montreal Canadiens have retired 18 nunbers, more than any other franchise.

29

The Detroit Red Wings have "Hockeytown" as part of their center ice logo.

30

The Tampa Bay Lightning go by the nickname Bolts.

31

The Florida Panthers are located the furthest south in Sunrise, Florida which is north of Miami.

32

The Washington Capitals have three stars in their logo.

33

The Dallas Stars and the Columbus Blue Jackets use a single star in their logos.

34

Which Canadian team is located the furthest to the east?

35

Which teams feature a single letter as a prominent part of the team logo?

34

The Montreal Canadiens are located furthest to the east of all the Canadian teams.

35

The following seven teams each feature a single letter in their logos:

Anaheim Ducks (D)
Boston Bruins (B)
Calgary Flames (C)
Colorado Avalanche (A)
Dallas Stars (D)
New Jersey Devils (N)
Philadelphia Flyers (P)

CATEGORY 3

HISTORY

36

When did the crease shape change from (2) to (3) as shown in the diagram below?

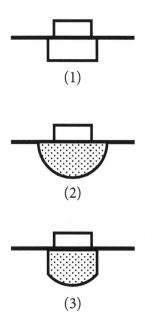

36

The crease shape was changed for the 1999-2000 season to version (3) in the diagram.

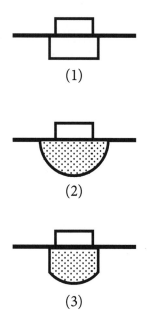

37

What is the Art Ross trophy awarded for?

38

When was the Zamboni invented?

39

What is inscribed on the Stanley Cup for 2005, the lockout year?

40

When did the NHL change from having the home team wear white jerseys to having the visiting team wear white?

41

What were the six expansion teams added to the NHL in 1967?

37

The Art Ross trophy goes to the player with the most regular season points.

38

The Zamboni was introduced in 1949 and a patent was awarded in 1953.

39

The inscription reads "2004-05 Season Not Played."

40

The switch to the home team wearing the colored jersey and the visitors wearing white was made in 2003.

41

The six teams added were the California Golden Seals, the Los Angeles Kings, the Minnesota North Stars, the Philadelphia Flyers, the Pittsburgh Penguins and the St. Louis Blues.

42

Where is the Hockey Hall of Fame located?

43

How many NHL teams are based in Canada?

44

In what US state was the Zamboni invented?

45

What uniform number will never be used again by any team?

46

When was the NHL created?

47

How many NHL teams were added after Wayne Gretzky went to the Los Angeles Kings?

42

The Hockey Hall of Fame is located in Toronto, Canada.

43

There are 7 Canadian NHL teams and 23 US teams.

44

The Zamboni was invented in California.

45

The NHL retired 99 to honor Wayne Gretzky.

46

The NHL was created in 1917.

47

Nine teams were added after Gretzky went to the Los Angeles Kings.

48

Which is faster, the fastest hockey shot or the fastest baseball pitch?

49

When did the NHL go to the shootout format for the regular season?

50

In the year 2015, were there more NHL teams or more MLB teams?

51

In what year did the number of NHL teams exceed 20?

52

What is a Gordie Howe hat trick?

48

The fastest recorded baseball pitch is 105.1 mph, while the fastest hockey shot recorded is 110.3 mph.

49

The shootout was introduced in the 2005-06 season.

50

As of 2015 there were 30 NHL teams and 30 MLB teams.

51

The number of NHL teams exceeded 20 in the 1979-80 season when the league expanded from 17 teams to 21 teams. The teams that were added were the Edmonton Oilers, the Hartford Whalers, the Quebec Nordiques and the Winnipeg Jets.

52

A Gordie Howe hat trick is a goal, an assist and a fight in the same game.

53

In the era of the Original Six from the 1942-43 season to the 1966-67 season , who won more cups, the two Canadian teams or the four US teams?

53

In the era from 1942-43 to 1966-67 the Canadian teams won 19 cups and the US teams won 6 cups.

CATEGORY 4

STADIUMS

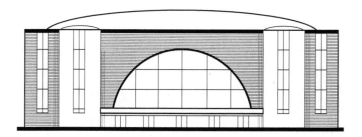

54

Which two stadiums do not bear the name of a corporate sponsor?

55

Which stadium is the newest?

56

Which stadium has the smallest seating capacity?

57

Which stadium has the largest seating capacity?

58

Which stadium besides Madison Square Garden has the word "Garden" in the name?

59

Which three stadiums are sponsored by airlines?

54
Joe Louis Arena in Detroit and Madison Square Garden in New York City are the only two arenas that are not named after a corporate sponsor.

55
The newest stadium is the Barclays Center, home of the New York Islanders. The Barclays Center opened in 2012.

56
The MTS Centre, home of the Winnipeg Jets, has the smallest seating capacity at 15,016.

57
The United Center, home of the Chicago Blackhawks, has the largest seating capacity at 22,428.

58
TD Garden in Boston is the other stadium with Garden in the name.

59
The three stadiums sponsored by airlines are the Air Canada Centre (Toronto Mapleleafs), the American Airlines Center (Dallas Stars) and the United Center (Chicago Blackhawks).

60

What are the three oldest stadiums being used today?

61

Which word, Arena or Center (including the spelling Centre), is used in more stadium names?

62

Which stadium does not have the red line overlapping the team logo?

63

Which team plays in the Bridgestone Arena?

64

Which team plays in the Canadian Tire Centre?

60
The three oldest stadiums are Madison Square Garden (New York Rangers), Rexall Place (Edmonton Oilers) and Joe Louis Arena (Detroit Red Wings).

61
There are 19 stadiums with Center in the name and 7 with Arena in the name.

62
The Bell Centre, home of the Montreal Canadiens, uses two logos with one on either side of the red line.

63
Bridgestone Arena is home to the Nashville Predators.

64
The Canadian Tire Centre is home to the Ottawa Senators.

65

Which team plays in PNC Arena?

66

Which team plays in the Xcel Energy Center?

65

PNC Arena is home for the Carolina Hurricanes.

66

The Xcel Energy Center is home for the Minnesota Wild.

CATEGORY 5

PLAYERS

67

Which four NHL teams did Wayne Gretzky play for?

68

Who scored more NHL goals, Bobby Hull or his son Brett Hull?

69

What is the record for goals scored in one season including playoff goals and who holds it?

70

Which two players have over 800 career goals?

71

Which three players have scored more than 80 goals in a single season?

67

Wayne Gretzky played for the Edmonton Oilers, the Los Angeles Kings, the St. Louis Blues and the New York Rangers.

68

Brett Hull scored 741 career goals, Bobby Hull scored 610 career goals.

69

Wayne Gretzky holds the record for most goals in a season including playoff goals with 100.

70

Wayne Gretzky (894) and Gordie Howe (801) both surpassed the 800 mark in career goals.

71

Wayne Gretzky (did it twice, with 92 and 87 goals), Brett Hull (86 goals) and Mario Lemieux (85 goals).

72

Who holds the record for most shootout goals in a season?

73

Which player has won the most Stanley Cups?

74

Which player has played in the most games including playoff games?

75

Who holds the record for most assists in a single period?

76

Who holds the career record for most short-handed goals?

72

Ilya Kovalchuck holds the record for most shootout goals in a season with 11 in the 2011-2012 season.

73

Henri Richard won 11 Stanley Cups.

74

Mark Messier played in 1992 games, including play-offs.

75

Dale Hawerchuck holds the record for most assists in a period with five.

76

Wayne Gretzky holds the record with 73 short-handed goals.

77

Who holds the record for the most shots on goal over a career?

78

Which goaltender holds the record for most wins in the playoffs?

79

Who holds the record for most regular season games played?

80

Who holds the record for most playoff powerplay goals scored?

81

Who has played in the most playoff games?

77

Ray Bourque holds the record for most shots on goal in a career with 6206.

78

Patrick Roy with 151 playoff wins.

79

Gordie Howe played the most regular season games with 1767 games played.

80

Brett Hull with 38 playoff powerplay goals.

81

Chris Chelios played in 266 playoff games, more than any other player.

82

Who holds the record for most penalty minutes in the playoffs?

83

Name eight teams that Jaromir Jagr has played for.

82

Dale Hunter with 729 playoff penalty minutes.

83

Jagr has played for the Pittsburgh Penguins, Washington Capitals, New York Rangers, Philadelphia Flyers, Dallas Stars, Boston Bruins, New Jersey Devils and Florida Panthers.

CATEGORY 6

PLAYOFFS

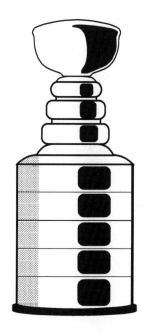

84

In the Original Six era 4 teams made the playoffs. Today 16 teams make the playoffs. During the expansion years, what other numbers of teams were used in the playoffs?

85

The Stanley Cup has been awarded every year since 1919 except one. Which year was the cup not awarded?

86

Which current teams have never made the finals?

87

How many times after 1980 did two Original Six teams make the finals?

88

How many timeouts does a team get if a game goes into overtime in the playoffs?

84

The league started using 8 in 1967-1968, then 12 in 1974-1975 and 16 in 1979-1980.

85

The cup was not awarded in 2005, the year of the lock out.

86

The teams below have not yet made the finals:

> Arizona Coyotes
> Columbus Blue Jackets
> Minnesota Wild
> Nashville Predators
> San Jose Sharks

87

After 1980 two Original Six teams met in the finals only once, in 2013 Chicago and Boston made the finals.

88

Each team gets only one time out for the entire game, including any overtime periods.

89

In what year did the playoffs first go to four rounds?

90

Since 1980 how many years featured two Canadian teams in the finals?

91

If two teams are tied for a division title in points, what are the first two tiebreakers used to decide a division title?

92

How many times since 1980 has a team won at least two cups in a row?

93

Which team most recently won three or more cups in a row?

89

The playoffs went to four rounds in the 1974-75 season when 12 teams made the playoffs. The four division winners got buys for the first round.

90

Just two years saw two Canadian finalists. The years were 1986 and 1989, and in both instances the teams were Calgary and Montreal.

91

The first tiebreaker is who has more regulation plus overtime wins (ROW), the second tiebreaker is points in head to head competition.

92

On five occasions since 1980 teams have won at least two cups in a row.

93

The New York Islanders, who won four in a row starting with the 1979-1980 season.

94

How many officials are on the ice during a playoff game?

95

The team winning the President's Trophy is granted what advantage in the playoffs?

96

How many rings are on the Stanley Cup?

94
There are four officials on the ice during the playoffs.

95
The winner of the President's Trophy will have home ice advantage in each series during its playoff run.

96
Three upper rings and five lower rings.

CATEGORY 7

NUMBERS

PTS	G	A	PPG	SHG
84	39	45	12	0
76	35	41	4	2
70	32	38	9	0
70	32	38	11	0
67	25	42	5	1
65	24	41	3	2
60	22	38	4	1
57	21	36	3	0
56	20	36	2	1
51	19	32	1	0

97

What are the differences in length and width of an NHL vs. international rink?

98

How many players can get an assist on any particular goal?

99

Wayne Gretzky is the all-time point leader. About how close is the number two player in career points?

10 points
50 points
100 points
500 points
1000 points
1500 points

97

The NHL rink is 200 feet long and the international rink is about the same at 61 meters or 200.13 feet. The NHL rink is 85 feet wide but the international rink is wider at 30 meters or 98.42 feet.

98

No assists can be awarded (unassisted goal) or as many as two.

99

Wayne Gretzky is the all-time leaader with 2857 career points, Mark Messier is second with 1887 points. The difference is about 1000 points.

100

How many points are awarded for a goal and how many for an assist?

101

How long would it take a shot going 100 mph to reach the net if shot from center ice?

102

Do shootout goals count in a goaltender's goals against statistics?

103

Does an empty net goal count against the goaltender's goals against statistics?

104

If a team had a perfect season, how many points would they have?

100

Both a goal and an assist are awarded one point.

101

The shot would need to travel 89 feet and would make it to the net in about .61 seconds.

102

No, shootout goals are not included in the goaltender's statistics.

103

No, the goaltender is not accountable for an empty net goal.

104

They would have 164 points, or two points each for 82 wins.

105

What kinds of penalties are assigned to each of the following numbers of penalty minutes?

2 minutes
4 minutes
5 minutes
10 minutes

106

How many people (including the timekeeper) need to fit in the penalty box?

107

How much time is there between periods?

105

2 minuttes - minor penalty
4 minutes - double minor
5 minutes - major penalty
10 minutes - misconduct

106

The penalty box needs to accomodate ten people, including the timekkeeper.

107

Time between periods is 18 minutes.

108

How wide are the blue lines and center red line?

109

How fast can professional hockey players skate?

> 15-25 mph
> 25-35 mph
> 35-45 mph
> 45-55 mph

110

How many goals are there in a natural hat trick?

111

If a player has 2 PPGs, 1 SOG and 1 OG how many points does he have?

108

The blue lines and center red line are twelve inches wide.

109

Professional hockey players can skate up to about 32 mph, so 25-35 mph is the correct range.

110

There are three goals in a natural hat trick. The "natural" hat trick occurs when the three goals are scored in succession by one player without any players on either team scoring in between.

111

He would have two points. The 2 PPGs (power play goals) each are awarded a point. The SOG (shootout goal) is not awarded a point nor is the OG (own goal).

Made in the USA
Las Vegas, NV
25 January 2022